Recovering Self-Worth
21 Life-Changing Actions

Jeannie E. Kelly

Copyright © 2018 Jeannie E. Kelly
All rights reserved.
ISBN: 0692934529
ISBN-13: 9780692934524

Back cover photo by Mary Clifton

Life Coach Services: email rsw21101@yahoo.com

Contents

About the Author

Jeannie Kelly was born in Mobile, Alabama, and raised in Sacramento, California, and then she moved to Sonoma County in her early twenties with her 3children. In 1989 she began her journey with the Lord. Later she met and married Michael Kelly in December 2000.

After fighting to discover who she was in Christ and learning to love herself, she accepted the call to encourage, equip, and strengthen others to have a healthy perception of self-worth.

In 1998, Jeannie began working first with teenage girls to encourage them to become all they were created to be. She held biweekly group meetings in her home on topics such as building self-esteem, discovering your talents, attaining educational success, and many others. Since then, she has spoken at different women's conferences and retreats.

In 2003, Jeannie and her husband moved to Lake County, California, where she still reside. She has been blessed with three children and twelve grandchildren and five great-grandchildren.
Recognizing all God had delivered her from—abuse, neglect, depression, low self-worth, and rejection—she began her work as a life coach.

Jeannie also enjoys writing, teaching, preaching, homesteading, and crafting. After nineteen years, it is still her passion to help others live their dream of knowing who they really are.

Dedication

This book is dedicated to those of you who have helped me to put on paper the words that were inside of me. I would like to acknowledge Mike for relentlessly pushing me to define my worth. To my children, Kristina, Tiffany, and David, thank you for the second chances you have given me. And to Jessica, thank you for encouraging me and helping me to stand when I was unable to stand on my own. My sincerest gratitude to Mary for all the time she has poured into the completion of this book. Without each of you, this would not have been possible.
Thank you.

By the grace of God I am what I am.

—1 Corinthians 15:10

Preface

I wrote this book for those who have suffered from a low opinion of self, as I have. It is for those who, like me, have danced to the song of "I will never be good enough." It is for those who have discovered self-worth is not something we can simply think into existence. We have tried and failed.

I have discovered that both love and self-worth are more than a feeling, and neither can exist without action. It has taken me the greater part of my life to love and embrace the person I am. I have diligently searched for love in any and every corner, only to be disappointed. I have tried to be what others wanted me to be and to think as others wanted me to think. Yet love and acceptance had consistently eluded me.

In this book, I am going to share with you twenty-one life-changing actions of recovering self-worth that I slowly but surely began to practice in my own life to gain and strengthen my self-worth. My hope for you, dear reader, is that you, too, will discover through the pages of this book a love and appreciation for yourself that you thought only existed for others.

Introduction

One of the things I enjoy doing is making crafts. I particularly like sewing and making soap. A few years back, I started selling my handmade items at different craft shows. I found it interesting to watch the expressions on some of the customers' faces as they would each pick up a piece and look with amazement at the detail in it. All along they were deciding what they were willing to pay. I, the artist, had already determined what the piece's value was. There were some who didn't think the piece was worth the set price. But their thoughts didn't change the value I had already placed on the piece. When they carefully set the piece back in its place and walked away, the value still did not change.

As the designer, I knew what it entailed to take a piece's creation from a thought to the finished product. I knew what materials needed to be used and the cost of them. I knew the conditions the product needed to be created in, and I was willing to invest the time it took to bring out the absolute best in the finished product.

I learned very early on that if I set a price too low, customers would think little of the product. Another thing I discovered while doing shows was I could have very similar pieces marked at different prices—say one at a lower amount of five dollars and another at fifteen. I would sell one or two of the lower-price items, and the fifteen-dollar items would sell well. When I took the same five-dollar product and marked it up to fifteen dollars, they sold like hotcakes. I realized I had to first determine the worth of my product. If I didn't see the value, the customers didn't see the value either.

Living life with low self-worth is like setting that five-dollar value on yourself. We go through life feeling overlooked and unworthy. We think ourselves second best. We harbor so many fears and hurts that keep us from enjoying everyday life.

Unlike a craft item, where the value is determined by cost and time, how do we determine our own value? Generally our conclusions on self-worth are based on our experiences and thoughts. If we derive our value based upon these, who would then be qualified to judge which experience is worthy and which is not, since there is no perfect person? How do we determine the value of people? It would stand to reason that we would have to go back to the Designer to see what value He placed on His creation. He is the only one qualified to determine its value.
The Designer said that you are fearfully and wonderfully made. *Psalm 139:14*

The Designer desired such a free-will relationship with us that He was willing to pay the high price for it—not as an owner for His own pleasure, but rather to give us a future and a hope. He wanted to be an ever-present help in our time of trouble. He took the brutal death on the cross on the off chance that we might want to have a relationship with Him. Even while on the cross, He knew He would never force you or me to have a relationship with Him. That is value. He paid the price just in case we might choose Him. He also paid the price out of love for us, love for His creation. Some of us may not have experienced much value. We might find it hard to believe that someone would place such a high value on us.

A one-hundred-dollar bill is still a one-hundred-dollar bill even if someone calls it a one-dollar bill. And if someone calls it a one-dollar bill, does the value change? What if that person treated it like it was a one-dollar bill and put it inside a change machine at the laundromat and received four quarters. He treated it like a dollar. Now imagine the owner of the coin machine finding that one-hundred-dollar bill in the machine. Did the value change? Sadly, some of us have been treated like that one-dollar bill, but this treatment does not determine our value. Even though the Designer has placed a high value on us, we must take action in order to reap its benefits.

At the end of each of the twenty-one principles discussed in this book, you will find a "Take Action" section. These are guided questions to help you turn the chapter's principle into an action.

It brings me great joy in thinking of the part, however small, that this book will play in helping you to finally lay down the damaging thoughts and behaviors that have kept you from allowing your light to shine.

Chapter 1

Self-Worth Is
to Stop Blaming Yourself

Lee Majors played the role of Colt Seavers in *The Fall Guy*, a popular TV show during the '80s. In this sitcom, he was a stuntman. In the show, whenever the star of the movie being filmed would have to do something dangerous, in would come the fall guy. He would take the fall, no questions asked. It was his job. He was trained to take the fall.

Those who struggle, or have struggled, with a low value of self take it upon themselves, like Colt Seavers, to be the fall guy for other people. We spend a lot of time training and perfecting the art of self-blame. Whenever something dangerous comes by way of others' choices, words, or actions, we come in and take the fall, no questions asked. It has been made our fault and we willingly accept the blame.

Because we do not live in a perfect world, bad things happen. The sad reality is that we as people are pretty selfish. We practice whatever it is that we have determined in our own eyes to be right. If we have justified a behavior, we continue to practice that behavior whenever it suits us or helps us fulfill our desires. Most often we are in pain and seeking relief. We don't stop to think how our actions will affect another person. And even if we do, justification comes in and tells us it is OK to do it anyway.

I say this because some of us have had so many bad things happen to us that we begin to play the role of Colt Seavers. We reason, "Because of who I am, I am getting what I deserve." The reality is that we are suffering the results of someone else's choices. Unfortunately, we sometimes end up in the direct line of the consequences of another's choice. It is not because of who you are. Rather, it is the power of choice. Bad things happen in life; you are not alone in this. At times I felt like I was alone. I believed other people had it so much better than I did. I thought their problems were minimal at best. That thought wasn't true, just like the "because-of-who-I-am, I-am-getting-what-I-deserve" thinking wasn't true.

We *all* have problems. They may be different, but they are still problems. That was one of the traps I constantly fell into. I would compare my life with someone else's, someone who I thought had it all. A few times I was granted inside information by way of a relationship with the person or his family, only to discover he was in as big of a mess as I was.

Selfishness doesn't care if you are a man, woman, boy, or girl. It doesn't care whether you are black, white, or in between. It doesn't care if you are rich or poor. Selfishness does what selfishness does. Selfishness blames you for its choices. It takes its best shot to devalue your worth. But one thing that selfishness cannot do is determine our value, unless we allow ourselves to believe that we are responsible for another person's actions. It can never take away your value without your permission. The Designer already determined your worth before any bad thing happened. He has already put His label on you.

Bad things happen because they just do. I am not minimizing your pain. Think of the things that just happen: cars break down, phones get dropped, people lose jobs, and kids make some really bad choices. Other people hurt us, things go wrong, and we also make bad choices. These are the speed bumps of life. But rest assured, you are not alone; bad things happen to each and every one of us. The key is learning how to respond to these things when they happen.

When we say it is our lot in life to receive one bad thing after another, we are saying it is our fault due to the person we are, because of the mistakes we made, and possibly the way we are treated. We believe we deserve it. That's just not true. The first action you should take is to stop blaming yourself for someone else's actions. We all have the gift of choice. This goes back to that free-will relationship.

Free will can seem like a double edged sword at times. We desire to be free to make our own choices and then blame others for the choices we've made. Or we want to rob others from that very freedom. When we take responsible for choices others make, we are robbing them of their life experiences, their processes of growth. There is freedom in love. Just as the Designer chooses to allow us to make our own choices even though He knew some of those choices would bring us a lot of pain, we must allow others the same freedoms.

We don't have power over other people. We cannot make anyone do or say anything, not even with our words or actions. Regardless of someone else's choices, we have value. So how do we know we have value? We know because the Designer placed it upon us.

"How great is the love the Father has lavished on us, that we should be called children of God!" 1 John 3:1

"'Though the mountains be shaken and the hills be removed, yet my unfailing love for you will not be shaken nor my covenant of peace be removed,' says the Lord, who has compassion on you." Isaiah 54:10

When we hit the speed bumps of life, we can begin to look at them as opportunities to do something different, to gain knowledge, and even to look for positive ways to use what we have gone through to help others who find themselves in like situations.

Take Action

Where are you taking responsibility for someone else's actions (that person's right to choose)?_____

_____

_____

_____

_____

_____

_____

_____

Without mentioning yourself, what is another reason the above behavior could have happened?

_____

_____

_____

_____

_____

_____

Chapter 2

Self-Worth Is
Letting Go of Regret

On the property where I live, I see a lot of wildlife. Being a homesteader, I appreciate raising, growing, and hunting our own food. One particular day, there were wild turkeys walking across the property, and my grandson said, "If Papa Mike could aim, we would have fresh meat." Needless to say, Papa Mike has never brought home any fresh meat other than from the grocery store. His weapon of choice, however, was a compound bow. Regret is like using that compound bow, a weapon of choice. But unlike Papa Mike, who couldn't hit the target, we use our weapon and hit the mark against ourselves every time. The sole purpose of this particular weapon is to blindside you with each passing day, to keep you from living, loving, and learning all that a moment can bring. Regret is our destiny killer.

We have spent many days regretting yesterday. All along, regret makes us miss this current day, week, and month, until finally another year has passed. We then are left with the regret of not having been strong enough to seize the time now passed, the time we could have spent being there for ourselves and others.

We continually say this year is going to be different: "Today I will take control and live my life." No sooner than this is said, we begin to remember the things we have done in the past, and regret once again is upon us. Like a deer in headlights, we freeze. The power of our yesterday is stronger than our will to live today. We feel trapped and immobilized by fear.

Occasionally, there are moments we are able to escape these self-erected prison walls and catch glimpses of joy and purpose, but we quickly retreat back to yesterday's guilt. But self-worth says bye-bye to regret and hello to fresh starts. We choose to use the lessons of yesterday for a profitable today.

Self-worth uses its yesterdays to become someone else's hope for today.

Take Action

Identify a regret you struggle with.

_____

_____

_____

_____

_____

What is one way you can use your regret to have a positive influence?

_____

_____

_____

_____

_____

Chapter 3

Self-Worth Is
Forgiving Yourself

Once again, peace has escaped me. Cindy is all grown up now, and I did the best I knew how when raising her. Through a series of bad decisions, she continues to hurt herself and others, and I blame myself for not being the person I should have been in her life when it mattered most. Had I been, I believe that she would not make the choices she is making today.

Why do we find it so much harder to encourage ourselves than we do other people? We find it easy to give an encouraging word to those who have struggled in the same areas we have. We tell them, "It's OK, you're not perfect, everyone makes mistakes," but we don't have that same grace for ourselves. When we don't show ourselves that same grace, we are saying to ourselves and the rest of the world, "I am above each of you. Out of all the people on the earth, I am the only one who is capable of living up to such a high standard. I am the only one who isn't allowed to blow it, to have made mistakes that hurt other people." This is an attitude of self-righteousness; it disguises itself as a victim but is actually pride.

Forgiving yourself is one of the biggest actions that will help you recover your self-worth. We all have a past. Even the one reminding you of your past has a past. If a person is constantly reminding you of your past, she might be a "toxic person." We'll talk more about toxic people in chapter 11.

Forgiving yourself is a part of accepting yourself. Self-acceptance will help you in your journey toward self-worth.

We are all a part of the human race, and humans are not perfect, including you. I don't use this as an excuse for us to live in any way that suits us. I say it so you can give yourself permission to lighten up and be kind to yourself, to recognize that we are no different with respect to making mistakes. A lot of us may have known better while making poor choices; again, we are human.

I may not know what you have done, but whatever it is, if you have done all you know to do to make a wrong choice/behavior right and have asked the Designer to forgive you and to help you do better, it's time to let it go. If you can't go back and change it, what purpose does it serve to keep you locked in this self-made prison? It's no one's childhood dream to grow up and mess up in a major way. Life happens to us and because of us. Self-forgiveness will free you to take hold of your destiny. Do not choose to continue walking hand in hand with condemnation. This is a vicious cycle in which those of us who struggle with self-worth will often contently dwell. We are the judge and jury of ourselves and have passed a joyless life sentence of unforgiveness toward ourselves. We replay scenes in our minds, wondering how we could have ever done *that*. The fact is, we did, and we cannot go back. But what we can do is move forward.

If you weren't the parent you should have been and your children are all grown up, you can't go back. After you have asked forgiveness, it's time to let it go and focus your time and energy on positive actions. We can take negative experiences from our pasts and use them for our benefit or someone else's benefit.

Using my example of weak parenting from my past, here is one idea for focusing your time and energy on something positive: You can learn what is to be the best grandparent ever. If you are not allowed to see your grandchildren or you don't have any, not to worry; there are so many children out there who need an adoptive grandparent. Or you may even find a single mom who could use what you have learned in your successes and failures as a parent. This does not take away your yesterday. Nor does it pay penance. But it does give you and others joyful moments and memories. Your grown children (like my Cindy) will find their way through self forgiveness as they watch you find yours. At one time we showed our children a negative example. Today however, we can choose to show them a positive example as we continue to walk in self forgiveness.

Take Action

Below, write down three areas you need to forgive yourself for. Answer each question honestly. The last step in this process is a little more difficult. It is an important action in recovering self-worth. Remember to be gentle with yourself.

1)_____

_____

_____

_____

Have you asked the person for forgiveness? _____

Have you asked the Designer to forgive you? _____

What would you tell someone who came to you hurting and broken over the same situation as your struggle? Write it here.

_____

_____

_____

_____

_____

_____

_____

_____

Take what you have written to a mirror and read the response to yourself.

2)_____

_____

_____

_____

_____

_____

Have you asked the person for forgiveness? _____
Have you asked the Designer to forgive you? _____

What would you tell someone who came to you hurting and broken over the same situation as your struggle? Write it here.

_____

_____

_____

_____

_____

_____

_____

_____

_____

_____

Take what you have written to a mirror and read the response to yourself.

3)_____

_____

_____

_____

_____

_____

Have you asked the person for forgiveness? _____
Have you asked the Designer to forgive you? _____

What would you tell someone who came to you hurting and
broken over the same situation as your struggle? Write it
here.

_____

_____

_____

_____

_____

_____

_____

_____

_____

Take what you have written to a mirror and read the
response to yourself.

Chapter 4

Self-Worth Is
Not Attaching a Mistake to Your Worth

I use to enjoy it when a store would make a mistake on the price of a product. The store would honor the mistake and sell me the item for the lower price and sometimes even give me a certain dollar amount. In retail that is great. But don't we do that to ourselves? When we devalue ourselves due to a mistake, our self-worth takes a dip. Our self-worth is already low, so when we make a mistake it is horrifying. The mistake confirms what we already believe to be true about ourselves. It proves that what others have said about us is true, and then we can tell ourselves a hardy "I told you so." Again we are putting ourselves in the "I'm the only one not allowed to make a mistake" category. The category no one else in the world is a part of.

But guess what? We are not alone. Mistakes are a part of discovery. Mistakes are a way of showing growth as you get better at something. Mistakes help us to see things differently. Mistakes say there is another way to accomplish our plan. So while we're thinking our mistake is another knock on our self-worth, it really is a launching pad for success. There is not one great person who has not made more mistakes than he can count. Thomas Edison, famous inventor of the light bulb, as well as the owner of over one thousand US patents, was asked about his failure to refine the light bulb after attempting to do so ten thousand times. He said, "I have not failed. I have just found ten thousand ways that won't work." In order to become great at any desired thing, it will take practice, practice, and more practice. Just like everyone else, we will have to keep trying until we strengthen that skill.

I used to want to just hurry up and accomplish whatever I was trying to do. I wanted to achieve perfection on my first try. I would give up and quit at the first sign of trouble or if it would end up taking a lot of time to correct the mistake. I would like to say I learned very quickly that giving up wasn't the way to go. But for me, struggling with my worth only caused every mistake to increase my lack of self-worth, and so I would quit.

I was attaching my mistakes to my overall value. Really, the two had nothing to do with each other. Once I practiced detaching my self-worth from all my mistakes, I took on a new view of the matter. I began to see failures as detours that brought knowledge. I learned to appreciate failures. Not that I was happy about them, but they no longer meant I was a failure. Believe me; I never thought I would see that day. I started to see how much knowledge I was gaining through my mistakes. When I once thought there was only one way to do something, I discovered there was a better way. I have to admit it, though; sometimes all those mistakes are downright frustrating, but then I remind myself of the last epic failure and what I walked away with. Failures are like a GPS; they just reroute you.

If you don't quit, you will get to your destination—although you come to discover that you never really arrive. There is so much more to learn through the journey to improve what it is you do or what you hope to do. I had to let go of the just-get-er' done mentality. You never stop learning and growing and improving. You get a little better each day. It's all about the journey. So let's just enjoy it.

Take Action

What is one mistake that you feel inadequate for making?

_____

_____

_____

_____

What did you learn from that mistake?

_____

_____

_____

_____

How can you use what you know now to help someone else?

_____

_____

_____

_____

Chapter 5

Self-Worth Is
Having Realistic Expectations of Yourself

Batman, Superman, Spiderman, and Wonder Woman were household names when I was growing up. I especially enjoyed laughing at my brothers and their friends as they set off to save the world inspired by an imaginary signal in the sky, leap over tall buildings in a single bound, or cut through walls of steel with their laser eyes. They completed their mission with all the pows, bams, and zaps needed to defeat the enemy. It makes for exciting play to take on the persona of a favorite superhero and save the day. But as children grow, their fantasies must be laid to rest (1 Cor. 13:11).

Self-worth cannot mature on fantasies. Recovering self-worth involves taking an honest look at what is on our plates and prayerfully removing what was not placed there by the Designer.

Oftentimes we take on more than we can or need to do. Are you familiar with the scripture that says God won't give you more than you can handle? (1 Cor. 10:13). Most of us have quoted this as we struggle with what we have perceived to be our responsibility. Perceptions can be wrong. What we say is that God's leading can really be our own reasoning and emotions. We are tired and burned out, and yet we continue to struggle with a load that we were never meant to bear. There are very good and noble things that need attention. The question is, is it our attention that is required?

When we see that we are unable to do all that we think we should be doing, we exchange the superhero mentality for feelings of unworthiness. We believe we ought to, and therefore we should be able to.

When we realize it is too much, instead of letting go of something, we often put an unspoken request on others around us. We reason, "They can see how much I have to do. Why don't they offer to help? Or better yet, just pitch in?" We justify these thoughts by reminding ourselves of when we have been there to help them. When these silent requests go unfulfilled, our self-worth takes another hit. We think, "If you cared for me, you would help me." We tend to think their lack of help equals a lack of worth toward self. It would be easy to slip into these thoughts: "I'm always the one there for everyone else, and no one is there for me." This is the victim mentality at its best. When you begin to have thoughts like these, it would be a great time to look over your gratitude list. You will begin to compile this list after chapter 9.

When we begin to sort through what is really our job and what is not, it is inevitable that there will be some things that we cannot simply quit cold turkey. Yet, with our new understanding, we can take steps to lessen the burden on our overloaded shoulders in all things.

I found it helpful to write down all that I was doing and then place them into one of three categories: (1) feelings/emotions, (2) destiny (your dream, your purpose) and (3) necessity. After I had my list, I would identify why I'd placed each one in its respective category. It helped me to be accountable for my own choices and actions. If I were allowing guilt to guide me, feelings/emotions, I had to take responsibility for that choice. Depending on the category, that would be a telltale sign of what I was truly supposed to be doing and what I thought I ought to be doing.

Another false expectation is thinking you should be further in life than you are. I had the privilege of working with a nineteen-year-old high school graduate who sincerely thought she should have accomplished more in life than what she had. Don't get hung up on her age of nineteen. Her lack of self-worth didn't start at nineteen. Had she allowed it to continue, she would be like most of us are today, struggling with self-contentment because the joyful feelings of doing well always lie within the thoughts of "only if." Only if I would have received a promotion, I would be happy. Only if I had received a higher grade, then I would know I am able. Only if I were not single, then life would be complete. Only if I had not made those mistakes, I would be much further than I am. The only ifs could go on and on. We can embrace and appreciate where we are today while setting reasonable goals for tomorrow. These same feelings that we share with her came from the same root, a lack of self-worth.

At nineteen she had her own apartment, car, and job and was attending college courses to become a psychiatrist. As she shared with me, it quickly became apparent she struggled with self-worth. As a child she felt she was not good enough, and her best efforts were considered unworthy of any praise. She was left at a young age to care for her siblings, and she was bullied relentlessly at school with no one to stand up for her. She often went without the basic necessities of life. She maintained an above-average

GPA and was still considered to be the reason for the family's dysfunction.

As we continued our weekly meetings, she slowly began to see, enjoy, and appreciate her accomplishments.

Our attempts at being superhuman are really attempts to make up for yesterday's perceived failures. The busier we are, the less time there is to think and feel.

Recovering self-worth requires you to stop judging yourself for not knowing how to do the things you were never taught to do. The acquired knowledge we have today is not the standard to be used in judging the past outcomes of yesterday.

Take Action

Put all the things you are doing into one of the three categories below. Really think about the feeling/emotion category. What seem like a necessity could really be your feelings. An example of this would be that caring for your young children is a necessity. On the other hand, caring for reasonably healthy adult children would be in the category of feelings/emotions.

Feelings/Emotions	Necessity	Destiny
_____	_____	_____
_____	_____	_____
_____	_____	_____
_____	_____	_____
_____	_____	_____
_____	_____	_____

When I was a child, I spake as a child, I understood as a child, I thought as a child: but when I became a man, I put away childish things.
—1 Corinthians 13:11 There hath no temptation taken you but such as is common to man: but God is faithful, who will not suffer you to be tempted above that ye are able; but will with the temptation also make a way to escape, that ye may be able to bear it.
—1 Corinthians 10:13

Chapter 6

Self-Worth Is
Having Patience with Yourself

One evening I was traveling back home from Santa Rosa. I was too tired to stop and get gas; I knew I had a little more than enough to make it home. The route home was a narrow, curvy mountain road. There was very little room to turn around, and it was dark. Shortly after reaching the area where I no longer had cell-phone reception, there stood a detour sign. Due to the winter weather, a tree had fallen across the road. I had no idea where the detour would take me.

Unfortunately, there is no easy loop or turnaround on a mountain. This was scary, to say the least. There weren't any houses that I could see. You don't find streetlamps on mountain roads to light the way, and very few cars were traveling at that time. I wasn't sure that I could make it with the amount of gas I had. This proved to be the longest detour ever, but I patiently continued on my drive.

Patience is the fuel to help us succeed. As we are learning to look at our mistakes and failures as knowledge in the making, we are going to need patience more than ever. You will have to remember to be kind to yourself. Like any new venture, it will involve trial and error.

Slipups and mess ups are bound to happen. Just remember that if you take one small step at a time, eventually you'll walk a mile. Having patience with yourself gives you the ability to turn an otherwise stressful, impossible situation into one with a doable outcome. I was forced to exhibit some form of patience while traveling that mountain road. It was a direction I had never gone before, and I didn't know where I was going to end up. But I had to keep going until I had nothing left—in the tank that is. Eventually I came across a familiar road, and fortunately I made it to my destination, thanking God all the way. When we set out to accomplish any task, we have to enter it with the mind-set of "No matter the detour, I'm going to continue until I have nothing left." With the tenacity of patience, we are able to make it to our destination and make that journey well. We are learning at every turn. We are persevering up every hill. Patience gives us an outcome worth smiling about.

Ever since I was a little girl, I've loved the idea of handmade anything. I wanted to be able to make Christmas gifts and my own garments. When I first began to take sewing lessons, I couldn't wait to get to the finished product. All I could focus on was the end result. I remember Janet, my sewing teacher, telling me over and over to slow down. I wanted to get to the finish line, and I wanted to do it right the first time around. If there was a shortcut, I wanted to find it. I did get to the finish line, but I wasn't pleased with the finished product. I quickly learned that if I didn't want to keep throwing away fabric I had to give myself a learning curve. I had to start at the beginning and learn techniques. I found myself frustrated a lot. The seam ripper and I became great friends. I had to learn what the tools were and how to properly use them. I had to learn what each machine foot was used for. I began to appreciate every right stitch, and doing something right took on a whole new meaning for me. This took time, but it was worth it. Now when I get to the finish line I am pleased with the outcome.

It takes time to become familiar with rerouting our actions and thoughts. It is OK to give yourself a learning curve. Patience is the way to success. Recovering self-worth is no different. It takes time to discover and appreciate who you are. Each time you do something different, celebrate your victory. Give yourself permission to feel pleased. When frustration begins to set in, take a break. Do something relaxing. Flip through a magazine, enjoy a glass of your favorite beverage, go for a walk, or think about your latest accomplishment (c'mon, you got them).

Practicing patience helps to keep you from becoming overwhelmed. Taking a moment to slow down and calm down will help keep things in perspective. Sometimes we just need to step back and regroup. We do not have to look at the whole picture. Practice looking at the immediate part of the picture. This is true for me when I'm writing a book; even though I have the words inside of me, it overwhelms me to think about the entire process. So I break the process into pieces. I find it easier to think of a chapter, or sometimes a page, a paragraph, or a sentence, than an entire book. And yes, I celebrate each piece I've done.

When you practice patience with yourself, you have more freedom to enjoy the process, and you have less stress. You have taken the burden of pressure to get things done quickly off your shoulders. With patience, those of us who are recovering our self-worth will no longer start and not finish projects. We will begin, and we will complete them. This is a great new adventure for us. Just like sewing, it takes every little stitch to finish the project.

Take Action

What is something you would like to do that seems too big or overwhelming?

_____

_____

_____

_____

_____

_____

Break it down into ten steps or less. (*If you need more steps, add more.*)

_____

_____

_____

_____

_____

_____

_____

_____

_____

_____

Set a start date_____

Chapter 7

Self-Worth Is
Being Honest

Have you ever said yes while thinking no? You're not alone. This was a go-to response for me. Resentment is a familiar building block for a lack of honesty. Wanting to please everyone is the mode of operation for those of us who are struggling or have struggled with our worth. We say yes when we mean no. We do not want to risk being rejected. With a strong desire to appear helpful and even needed, we say yes while we are shaking our head no on the inside. The problem with this is no one knows we are thinking no but us.

Many times, even while the word *yes* was coming out of my mouth, I could feel resentments building inside me and adding onto the other unresolved issues I was carrying around within me. I would blame the other person for asking and myself for offering. I was caught in a vicious cycle. If I were to say no, I would always wonder, "Had I said yes, would I have been really accepted by the other person?"

The word *really* is a favorite adverb for people struggling with self-worth. "Do they really like me? Do they really want me around? Do they really want to be with me? Do they really love me?" Are any of these sounding familiar? We are already accepted, loved, and wanted by others. But we see through the eyes of that low five-dollar value. As long as we have placed a low value on ourselves, we will naturally think others see us in the same way.

Resentment comes in when we fail to use our words. When we don't express how we feel about something, ask for help when we need it, or set boundaries regarding the way we are spoken to or the way we are treated. We blame the other person for not being able to read our minds. We rationalize that "she should know this and how it makes me feel." Remember, we have inside information that we have not allowed others in on. Practicing using our words is a must in gaining self-worth. Honesty also calls for us to take a different look at situations that have happened over the years and to take ownership over our part—not the part of others, just the part we played in it.

I do want to clarify: children who have been abused by adults, have no part in the abuse. Adults today are not responsible for the abuse they underwent as a child. When taking an honest look, some adult situations may not have a part. The key here is honesty.

This can be quite difficult. If you are like me, you have spent the better part of your years seeing an event one way, and to challenge what you have perceived to be true is frightening. In this process, all that we have built our belief system on is being challenged. When we challenge our thoughts, not only do we have to take proper action, but we have to admit that we may have misunderstood what happened. While we may fight the idea of being wrong, this admittance leads to the recovery of self-worth. It allows us once again to accept our humanity. As we begin to see things clearly, we have to take responsibility for our words and our actions.

When we initially experienced the situation, we took the action needed to protect ourselves. In a sense we will still be doing that. Only this time, with the new information gained, we will take the proper actions of renewing our minds (to think differently) about the situation(s) and learning how we can use this new information for the betterment of our self-worth.

Take Action

What are two things you are famous for saying yes to when you really mean no?

1)_____

_____

_____

2)_____

_____

_____

Write out a brief statement for each, saying no kindly.

1)_____

_____

_____

2)_____

_____

_____

Tell about two times you had misunderstood a situation.

1)_____

_____

_____

How do you see it differently now?

_____

_____

_____

2)_____

_____

_____

How do you see it differently now?

_____

_____

_____

Chapter 8

Self-Worth Is
Taking Responsibility

Recently I was waiting my turn to be served at a restaurant, and a gentleman came in just beaming. His clothes were dirty, his hair unkempt, and some teeth were missing. He shared with me how he had just spent the day working eight hours. The eight-hour shift was in no way the sole cause of his overall appearance. He, by the sweat of his brow, though, was able to walk in and have his order taken. The events that had led to his appearance weren't important to him. What was important was that he took responsibility for his part in being able to walk in and enjoy a meal that he was able to pay for, and he felt great about it. He was dripping with self-worth.

Have you ever noticed the pride you feel when you have taken ownership of a purchase made or an action taken? This can be anything from paying the electricity bill to honoring a commitment. We stand a little taller when we know it is due to our efforts that we are able to put food on the table or simply when the house is clean because that is what we said we were going to do that day.

Failing to take responsibility is like a computer virus. It has the ability to copy this same behavior to other areas of our lives, thus keeping us in a victim state. Taking responsibility cleans our mental space.

The gentleman in line at the restaurant exhibited the side of taking responsibility that is often overlooked. We usually are familiar with the negative side of ownership, being responsible for our actions or words. But the other side of the coin is the one that brings freedom. It is when we ask forgiveness for doing wrong to someone or when we also look at the part we played that brought harm to us. When we take responsibility for our part, we begin to release the victim mentality. There is a sense of pride that comes with it. That's not to say there won't be consequences for some of our actions, but our overall mental, emotional, physical, and even spiritual health could be much improved with taking responsibility in all areas, especially those that bring a pleasant outcome.

Taking responsibility can save us a lot of heartache and discouragement. When we begin to take action, we will find taking responsibly for our actions isn't as scary as it once appeared. So far in our journey, we have accepted that we are not superhuman. We have accepted that we are all on the same playing field when it comes to slipups and mess ups. We have learned the importance of being gentle with ourselves and appreciating the learning curve instead of fearing it. Most important, we have learned that taking responsibility by admitting to a wrong doesn't change our value.

For those of us who have attached a mistake to our very worth, every time we admit wrongdoing we use it as a confirmation of our unworthiness instead of claiming the freedom it is supposed to bring. I remember many years ago I was with a friend, and a song came on the radio. Well, I sang the lyrics wrong. My friend told me what the words were, and I was humiliated. I felt incredibly stupid. I had stepped out of my comfort zone, just a bit, and made a huge fool out of myself, or so I thought. But instead of just admitting that I had made the mistake and laughing it off, I lied and said that her version was what I had sung. That became the longest car ride ever.

When you have journeyed through life without; love, value, or acceptance, your worth is easily attached to the very simplest of mistakes, even that of a song. Those small molehills become huge mountains of confirmation. We tend to determine the value of our worth "when I…" "if I…" or "because I…," but our value isn't attached to any of these actions. It is because the Designer, the One who created us, gave us His seal of approval and stamped us with value, period. There is no *when*, *if*, or *because.* In His eyes it's just *period.*

Take Action

What are three positive outcomes you can take responsibility for?

1)_____

_____

_____

_____

_____

_____

2)_____

_____

_____

3)

Chapter 9

Self-Worth Is
Making a Daily Gratitude List

Yes, I know I woke up in the morning. That was the number-one phrase I heard when others were trying to give me something to be grateful for. I never really understood that saying. When you struggle with self-worth, facing the day can be pretty grim. We muddle through at best and go to bed feeling guilty that we did not accomplish much. We once again missed the opportunity to discover the beauty of the day in our own worth, not to mention being emotionally unavailable for those depending on us. The feelings of "why bother" creep into our minds.

I had grown so accustomed to the negative I could no longer see anything positive. I had to ask the Designer to give me eyes to see what I had to be grateful for. That may sound silly, but it was where I was at. The Designer didn't treat me like an ungrateful brat. Rather, He helped me to see all I had to be grateful for even in the midst of my struggle. As my eyes started to open, I began to notice things I couldn't see before. I finally had some things that I could write down on my gratitude list!

There were times I would forget to keep my list going—bad habits are hard to break—but I simply would give myself permission to begin again. Recovering self-worth takes practice. We start healthy habits, and we stop. But to start again is one of the keys to recovering self-worth.

Being grateful opened my eyes to see positive things to which I had previously been blinded by negativity.

I was able to take notice of the little things. I was grateful to sit outside in the cool of the day. I was grateful that I had begun to dream again. Over time I was grateful that I wasn't as fearful as I once was. I was grateful for second chances. The number-one thing I was grateful for was—drum roll please—I woke up in the morning. Yes, I woke up in the morning. I realized it wasn't as much about the waking up as it was about the opportunity that waking up brought. It allowed me to catch a glimmer of not only my worth, but my purpose as well. If I didn't wake up, there would be no hope at all. At least by waking up there was hope of doing something different. And as I continued to recover my worth, different was becoming the new familiar.

My early gratitude list was very simple, but over time I found it easier to see the many reasons I had to be grateful. Here were a few things from my first list:

1. There are people in my life who encourage me.
2. My car is running.
3. My bills are paid, and I have food.
4. I'm starting to believe that the Designer loves me.
5. I have hope.

Every list will be unique because you are unique. Put something on your list every day. If you are having a hard time thinking of what to be grateful for, don't worry—I won't tell you "you woke up this morning." Ask the Designer. If He showed me, He will show you. Before long you will see so many reasons to be thankful. As you do, you will experience the gratitude that recovers self-worth.

Take Action

For the next seven days, write down one thing you are grateful for each day.

_____   _____

_____   _____

_____   _____

_____

Chapter 10

Self-Worth Is
No Longer Comparing Yourself to Others

Betty went for a walk through the park. As she walked, she noticed how nice a lady's hair looked. She thought to herself, "If only I had hair like that, I would be able to do so much more with it." As she continued her walk, she ran into her friend, Debbie. She left Debbie thinking, "If I had her nose, it would be more proportioned with my face and improve my overall appearance." As she was finishing her walk, she stopped at the crosswalk where she saw Karen sitting at a stoplight in her fancy sports car. She thought, "If I had a career like Karen's, I would really be complete." By the time she had returned home, she had manufactured a whole new person with fabulous hair, a great nose, and an incredible career. Betty was quite satisfied until she went for a walk the next day.

How many of us can relate to Betty, where we think the grass is always greener on the other side? We look through rose-colored glasses at others and what they have, not realizing the weeds still have to be pulled and the grass still needs to be mowed, even on the other side.

We, by unique design, were created with everything we need to thrive, enjoy, achieve, and appreciate the person we are. We are fearfully and wonderfully made, and we stand second to no one except to God alone. We are no less in value than the next guy.

Coco Chanel, a famous designer, was the sole creator of the DKNY label (Donna Karen New York).

Since then, this label has seen many new additions in the fashion segment. Chanel is noted as saying, "In order to be irreplaceable, one must always be different."

The very thing that sets us apart is the very thing we are trying to change. It is our uniqueness that causes our light to shine the brightest. If Coco Chanel understood this principle as she created her fashions, how much more would the Designer Himself create us to be different? Self-discovery is a wonderful thing. You begin to notice things you really enjoy doing and things you are good at. You start to notice things you like about your physical appearance. You begin to see the beauty of you. All those hidden talents start to appear. You start to notice the little things, like your favorite color.

I just happened upon my favorite color one day. For the longest time, my favorite color was always someone else's favorite color. It was purple because of Prince and *Purple Rain*. It was yellow because it was my mother's favorite color.

One day I was looking through my closet, and I noticed most of my clothes had green tones. As I walked through my house, more green. That's when I realized green is my favorite color.

As we take the time to get to know ourselves, we see that there are so many wonderful things about us that it is not necessary to try to be someone else. Self-worth strives at being authentic. It is your authentic self who will soar to great heights. And your height is not the height of someone else. And this is why authenticity is so important. If we constantly look at others, we may very well miss our own mark.

Betty was creating a Frankenstein. Anytime we are out to change ourselves to be like someone else, we are working in the lab. The more I get to know me, the less I want to be them. That's not to say I haven't met some great people. There are people I admire, but I no longer want to mold myself into them. Give yourself permission to embrace who you were designed to be.

Take Action

What is your favorite color?

_____

What is your favorite food?

_____

What do you enjoy doing?

_____

Where do you like to go?

_____

What are you good at?

_____

What ten great qualities do you like about yourself? Be honest—you have them.

_____

_____

_____

_____

_____

_____

_____

_____

_____

Chapter 11

Self-Worth Is
Walking Away from Toxic People

The Skull and crossbones is a universal sign of danger. It is the picture on the bottle of lye that I use to make soap. We see this and know to keep it out of the reach of children as well as to handle it with care. If only people had this same universal sign on them to warn us.

Walking away from toxic people is one of the actions I found to be more difficult in recovering self-worth. How do I walk away from what and who is familiar? The toxicity that I received from others is what I believed to be true about myself. Due to this belief system, I allowed others to treat me poorly. It may have been toxic, but I learned how to live with it. It was toxic, but I made excuses for it. When I was finally able to be honest with myself, I realized that I thought I deserved to be treated badly.

Breaking the habit of toxicity takes work. I experienced a lot of uncomfortable feelings that come with breaking any addiction. I would walk away for a time, and then I would tell myself it was easier to just deal with the situation, so I would return to it once again. It didn't take me long to remember why I did not like it, and I would try again to break the habit. Yes, it had become a habit to accept the way others saw me as truth, whether it came through in their words or how they treated me.

I had to practice being gentle with myself while learning to break habits. Do not despise small steps when breaking a habit. For me to do anything cold turkey was extremely difficult. There were times when cold turkey was the only way to go, but other times one small step after another was all I could do to reach a level of success I had not previously seen.

I had started a new job and hadn't been there very long. I quickly learned my boss was very critical. I kept telling myself it was my boss's issue, not mine. I repeated this over and over. It had gotten to the point that I would say it to myself before the boss checked my work.

One evening at work, I finally couldn't take it anymore. I went into the bathroom and cried. I couldn't understand why this had affected me so much. I barely knew the person, and I could see his bitterness, pain, and fear. I knew it had nothing to do with me, and yet it had affected me so deeply. While in the bathroom crying, it came to me—I wasn't upset because of this person. I was upset because I had allowed a person with whom I'd lived in the same home for over fifteen years to criticize me almost daily. No matter what I had done, it was never good enough, and I was always at fault. I became responsible for this person's emotional well-being at the cost of everything about me. My boss was the catalyst I needed to see the damage done and to start making the necessary changes for my own sense of well-being.

It was at that point that I began to limit my interactions with those who were critical of me, those who constantly found fault in me. I stopped taking some of the phone calls. I wouldn't hang out as much. I spent less and less time with them. While I was doing this, I had little windows of opportunity to see the difference in my thought process these changes were making. I began to have a few positive thoughts. Slowly but surely I began to think "I can." I found that as I limited my time spent with toxic people outside my tight circle, I could start coming up with ideas to protect my emotional well-being from the ones who were within my circle.

Exercise was one form of release for me. I would go for walks or do stretches. I know it doesn't sound like much, but it was. It was a small step toward recovering my self-worth.

I would also write down one thing I was grateful for every day (chapter 9). I quoted scriptures about how the Designer saw me, and I read books on gaining a healthy self-image. As I continued these practices, I was able to set and enforce boundaries with all who were critical of me. Including those in my inner circle.

Take Action

What are two ways you could limit time spent with toxic people in your life?

1)_____

_____

_____

2)_____

_____

_____

What are three healthy ways you could free up your mental space? For example, exercise, journaling.

1)_____

_____

_____

2)_____

_____

_____

3)_____

_____

_____

Chapter 12

Self-Worth Is
Forgiving Others

Hornworms and tomato plants just don't mix. While on my homestead, I grew all types of vegetables. I was given the opportunity to learn how to can tomatoes and make spaghetti sauce. (That ruined store-bought spaghetti sauce for me!) I planted twenty-four tomato plants. I knew I would need a lot of tomatoes in order to put up enough sauce to last until the following season and to be able to bless friends with a jar. One day while out watering my garden, I noticed a hornworm on one of my tomato plants. I had never seen one before and thought it interesting that it blended in so beautifully with the plants. The worm was the same color as the stems. I just happened to notice them for the first time. As I continued to water, I saw another one. After doing some research, I discovered they were not the friendly sort of insect for my plants. If they would have continued to go undetected, my tomato plants would not have produced what they were intended to produce. In fact, the plants might have been destroyed altogether. Those worms would have eaten away at the very thing I wanted to harvest. Needless to say, they became a treat for my chickens.

Unforgiveness is like those hornworms. After a while it begins to blend in so perfectly with our character that it becomes hard to detect. Like my tomato plants, our personal growth can only go so far before unforgiveness's destruction manifests. If we are not careful to forgive when a situation arises that bears the resemblance of yesterday's pain, unforgiveness and its telltale signs of anger, resentment, and bitterness will be unleashed on some poor unsuspecting soul.

Forgiveness is a gift we give ourselves. Holding on to an offense, as deserving as the offender may be of unforgiveness, only serves to eat away at us like the hornworms to tomato plants. As long as we are holding on to this, we will never produce what we were planted to produce. Sure, we will have accomplishments, but we will only get so far before yesterday shows up to rob us of our peace.

Forgiveness is another action that lays down the victim mentality. Forgiveness frees up our mental space and enables us to explore our dreams. We are no longer wasting our energy on what we do not have the power to change. Forgiveness says that we are learning to value ourselves and yesterday's pain can no longer stand in the way of today's hope.

Through our journey in recovering self-worth, we are learning that mistakes are just a big part of life. We are going to make them, and they are going to be made against us. The sooner we let go and let God, the sooner we can return our focus to the things that matter most, like producing what we were planted to produce.

Take Action

Our messes may be different, but they have one thing in common—they're still messes.

List five people you want to be, or have been, forgiven by.

_____

_____

_____

_____

_____

List five people you need to forgive. Forgiveness is for your emotional freedom.

_____

_____

_____

_____

_____

Write one or two sentences forgiving those whom you named above.

1)_____

_____

_____

_____

2)_____

_____

_____

_____

3)_____

_____

_____

_____

4)_____

_____

_____

_____

5)_____

_____

_____

_____

Chapter 13

Self-Worth Is
Showing Respect to Others

Bullying is becoming more prevalent—it's a silent killer of its victims, either by tearing down lives or demolishing self-worth. So many young people are being destroyed over what is considered a natural experience of growing up. Our children should not have to hide out while at school or skip school to keep from being bullied. All too often, the bullied child grows up to become the very thing she despised. Bullying is the fear of the tormentor. It seeks to kill the soul and take the life out of its prey. People are treated as circus animals: something to be controlled by any means necessary.

There is no place for manipulation or bullying, and there is definitely no place for a child putting her hands on another human being in order to have her way.

Manipulation is a feeble attempt to get what you believe you need or want from another person. The need may be real, but if obtained in a questionable manner, we really do ourselves a disservice, because what we received was not freely given. We then doubt if what was received was genuine. As long as we doubt, we continue to bully. This ultimately will keep us in a self-loathing fight on the inside that is reflected in how we treat others on the outside.

Since we constantly have to use manipulation as a way to obtain a desired outcome, it continues to reaffirm the lack of value we have for ourselves. We then assume others see us in the same light. We reason, "If I had value, the things I seek would be freely given, but since I do not have any value, I must take what I want from you." As long as we continue in these behaviors, we will never know how sweet it is to have "it," whatever it may be, freely given to us.

When we no longer have to make it happen and we find ourselves receiving "it" freely, we are then able to rest and enjoy "it" from those who choose to give it. We recognize and accept that not everyone will choose to give "it," and that is each person's choice. Though it may hurt our feelings, we understand that the choice is not attached to our value. We know that we will survive and continue to live our lives and pursue our goals.

As we allow "it" (whatever we are wanting from another human being) to happen of its own free will, the behaviors that once promoted self-loathing will begin to subside. As we will see in the next action, we don't need to bulldoze other people in order to feel good about ourselves. Running over others is just another telltale sign of the lack of value we have placed on ourselves.

People with a healthy self-worth do not find they need to tear other people down, in word or deed, in an attempt to control them. During this journey of recovering self-worth, we learn to appreciate our own uniqueness, and in doing so, we are no longer jealous, controlling, or envious of other people for the uniqueness they possess. We realize we don't have to have certain people in our lives to be whole, complete, or happy. We don't punish other people because of their gifts and talents or the people they are. Rather we focus our attention on sharpening our own tools. We are happy to search out, through trial and error, ways to utilize our own gifts and talents.

Take Action

Give three reasons why someone may bully another.

1)_____

_____

_____

_____

_____

_____

2)_____

_____

_____

_____

_____

_____

3)_____

_____

_____

_____

_____

_____

List three ways of bullying.

1)_____

_____

_____

_____

_____

_____

2)_____

_____

_____

_____

_____

_____

3)_____

_____

_____

_____

_____

_____

Do you think control plays a role in bullying?

_____

If yes, why? If no, why not?

_____

_____

_____

_____

_____

_____

What would you say to a person who is or has been bullied?

_____

_____

_____

_____

_____

_____

What do you think a bully should do instead of bullying? How would the bully accomplish this?

_____

_____

_____

_____

You are fearfully and wonderfully made. No one controls your destiny, and no one has the right to treat you any way he or she sees fit. You are a very special creation, created for great things. You, my dear reader, are an extraordinary human being. Human words and actions cannot take away from or give you your value. You are dearly loved and valued because the Designer Himself believed you were worth dying for. And so He did. There is no greater love than a friend laying down His life for you.

I will praise thee; for I am fearfully and wonderfully made: marvelous are thy works; and that my soul knoweth right well
—Psalm 139:14

For God so loved the world, that he gave his only begotten Son, that whosoever believeth in him should not perish, but have everlasting life.
—John 3:16

Greater love hath no man than this, that a man lay down his life for his friends.
—John 15:13

Chapter 14

Self-Worth Is
Sharing Your Opinion While Not Being Opinionated

Have you ever witnessed a one-person conversation? You know the type, where two or more people are present but one person has set the stage, only allowing his voice to be heard and steamrolling any other opinion. Unfortunately, these actions have stopped others from hearing his point of view. It is not that the others don't want to hear his words; he has just chosen for the others in the conversation to hear his actions instead, and not his viewpoint, by his method of delivery.

When we struggle with self-worth, we may find it difficult to convey our opinion to others without seeming overbearing. Between the passion of your opinion, your nerves, and your rising fear of speaking to other people, especially in a group setting, it can be unsettling to say the least.

In fear of not being heard and not having our opinion respected, we tend to drive the point home, even if that means not allowing others to have or share their opinion. "If you don't accept what I am saying, then you don't understand my point. If you don't receive my point, then something must be wrong with me."

It's a setup created by our wounded soul. People with low self-worth have been hurt in so many ways that they have become thin skinned. We are easily offended due to our own misconceptions of our worth. We tend to bulldoze others. Bulldozing is used as a self-protection tool to keep people at arm's length. Due to bulldozing, people tend not to want to be around us, and therefore we keep ourselves safe from possible ridicule. We subconsciously set ourselves up to remain isolated. We have wrongly attached our worth to whether or not others agree with us. We think, "I would rather close off your opinion than to be reminded of what I believe to be true of myself."

Self-worth recognizes that we are all uniquely different and have different points of view. We all process and see information differently, leading to different opinions. Your worth is not attached to your argument, nor is it attached to the arguments presented by others.

I found this exercise helpful while learning to hold respect for those with a different opinion from mine. Once I shared my opinion, I would listen to the other person without interrupting, and I didn't always present a rebuttal, which did not mean I agreed with her view. I realized I didn't need to fight to prove anything. Instead, I am learning to welcome different points of view while embracing my own opinion.

The other side of a conversation is speaking up even when you do not hold the same view as others. Not only does self-worth speak with respect toward others, it also has a voice. Self-worth knows that your opinion is just as valid as the next guy's, though they may differ. We can all learn something through conversation. Because we are always learning, opinions are no more written in stone than goals are. Like goals, they can be modified, or changed, as new knowledge is gained. Just because we start out in one direction doesn't mean we have to finish in the same direction. To have a change of heart is not defeat or weakness; it is growth and revelation of knowledge. And that is the end result we are seeking.

Take Action

What is a topic you are passionate about?

_____

_____

_____

_____

What feelings and emotions come up as you share your opinion?

_____

_____

_____

_____

_____

_____

With this topic, are others actively engaged with you in conversation? _____

If not, what steps can you take to let others know their opinion matters?

1)_____

_____

2)_____

_____

3)_____

_____

Do you tend to keep your opinion to yourself?

_____

If so, what goes on with your body, feelings, and thoughts when you think of sharing?

_____

_____

_____

_____

_____

_____

Where are three places you can practice sharing your opinion?

1)_____

_____

2)_____

_____

3)_____

_____

Chapter 15

Self-Worth Is
Asking for Help

You know the ongoing joke that has lasted the test of time: a man will never stop and ask for directions. If it means asking for help, men would rather drive around in circles than reach their destination in a timely fashion. We poke fun at men, yet how many of us have been circling the same mountain with the same thoughts as the "I will do it myself, man!"

We were created for relationships. As scary as that may seem, we were created to thrive and exist with one another. Asking questions embraces our humanity and recognizes our limitations. Asking for help is one aspect of relationships. But all too often, pride gets in the way of our asking for help. We secretly believe that we are less than others if we can't figure something out. We consider ourselves not to be up to par if we don't gain the necessary understanding right away. We would rather allow an opportunity to go by than to risk being thought of as stupid or inadequate. We fear being laughed at. These actions confirm what we already think to be true about ourselves.

As previously discussed, we need to grant ourselves a learning curve as we attempt new things. Asking for help is the direct opposite of these prideful thoughts. Asking for help says, "I don't know it yet, but I will." It says, "I realize I can't do this by myself, but I will play a part in getting it done." Through asking for help, we see that we are not alone.

Living independently of one another is not living. Rather it is doing the very thing we really don't want. Everyone wants to be accepted. When we ask for help, it shows our vulnerability, which causes our defenses to come down. When our defenses come down, we allow others to see our true self, in a sense; we are inviting others to step right on into our mess.

When we ask for help in different areas, different parts of us are no longer hidden. Our fear, our lack of understanding, our lack of articulateness, and our lack of know-how on an array of different things all come into focus. It is the price for community. This is frightening, especially if vulnerability has equaled pain and shame in the past.

Along with all of the fears that will be known, all that we have to offer the community will also be known. As we become known, you may be called upon to help in an area where you shine. That is what community is, the sharing of each gift to benefit the whole. But as long as we are justifiably content with being hidden, we fight the very thing we want most, relationship. Recovering self-worth is an action. Each time we practice allowing our true self to manifest, our mind-sets change. Our eyes begin to open to those who are willing to help us. We discover there are those who really are for us. We don't have to continue to let fear keep us living a life of independence.

No one ever arrives at having all knowledge. We will always need help from time to time. Whether we ask for help in learning how to do something or carrying furniture, our self-worth rises because we recognize and accept that we, just like others, will never stop learning and that we need one another.

Take Action

What is something you would like help doing?

_____

_____

_____

_____

What risk would you be taking by asking for help?

_____

_____

_____

_____

If asking for help went the way you hoped, what would be the positive outcome?

_____

_____

_____

_____

Chapter 16
Self-Worth Is
Trying New Things

Several years ago my husband and I took a youth group to Cummins, California, for a team-building wilderness experience. Having a new outlook on failure makes trying new things a breeze. Coming into the understanding of our worth has nothing to do with success or failure but has everything to do with being created by the Master Designer Himself. With this information, we have nothing to lose and everything to gain. The experience is worth gaining. One day it's going to be a story worth telling.

Once we arrived, I was very excited to float down a gentle flowing stream on an inner tube. That's what the pictures looked like when I signed us up.

Our first exercise was a two- to three-mile hike along an up-and-down mountainside. I managed to get through that even though I was a lot slower than the others. At the end of this hike, we came to the body of water we had to swim across to the next destination. Seriously, where's the gentle flowing stream? The inner tubes quickly turned into two-liter soda bottles, and those were only given out if absolutely necessary. And did I mention there were snakes swimming in the water?

When we eventually arrived at our destination, there was a huge rock in the middle of this river. We rested there on top of the rock. It was an experience.

The following day we were introduced to rock climbing. I did that OK. And then we hiked some more.

When we came to a cliff, we were told we would be very excited to get to the bottom, that something breathtaking awaited us. I was super excited to reach the destination. What would be this sight we'd behold? With all the anticipation of reaching the place, I failed to realize how I was getting there. We all kind of scooted down this terrain. As I was making my way down, I forgot to think about how I was going to get back up. Once at the bottom, it was the most beautiful place I'd ever seen. The water was crystal clear, and some of the children were baptized there. It gave me such joy to see the teens having such a great time jumping off rocks into the magnificent oasis. Eventually the time came to make our way back to camp. This is where the fun really began. We had to become a human ladder to help one another to scale an approximately seventy-five degree mountain. We had to climb on top of one another to get back up. And if you were to fall, you would fall into the river with rocks. Yep, it was an experience. Needless to say, I was terrified. The boys saw my fear and began to encourage me while each one, in turn, held on to me. It was the most amazing thing to watch these teenage boys lay down selfishness and transform before my eyes into valiant young men. It gives me such joy to share this experience. Make no mistake, I won't do it again, but I am so glad I tried something new.

The beauty of trying new things is that they can cause you to begin to dream again. We can finally start checking off that once-forgotten list of things we wanted to do but thought we could never do. While doing a new thing, we see all that we are made of. Today we are learning, no matter what, that we can try.

Trying new things is the very essence of living. Life is made up of experiences. Recovering self-worth means no longer denying ourselves the experiences life brings. It is enjoying life and life to the full. It is seizing opportunities that present themselves. It adds another color to the portrait of you. Trying new things also brings self-discovery. We learn what we like, who we are, and what we are capable of. They teach us what we don't like and what we no longer choose to tolerate. It really is an adventure that breaks up the humdrum of everyday life that we can sometimes fall into.

A new experience is like a child at Christmas; it is exciting to have something to look forward to, to have the anticipation of what may come. We know we do not need to have all the answers before we try, because no matter the outcome, we are more than capable of handling it.

Take Action

What are two things you would like to try that don't take a lot of money?

1)_____

_____

_____

_____

What is keeping you from trying?

_____

_____

_____

_____

_____

What do you need to do to prepare for this new thing?

_____

_____

_____

_____

_____

_____

Set a date to try._____

2)_____

_____

_____

_____

What is keeping you from trying?

_____

_____

_____

_____

What do you need to do to prepare for this new thing?

_____

_____

_____

_____

_____

_____

Set a date to try._____

Chapter 17

Self-Worth Is
Trying Again

Oprah Winfrey was fired from her first TV job as an anchor. Today she owns her own show. Steven Spielberg was rejected twice by the University Southern California School of Cinematic Arts. The very school that rejected him ended up erecting a building in dedication to him. Jim Carrey was booed off stage. Over one thousand people rejected Colonel Sanders's chicken recipe. These are just a few of the many who have had to endure failure and ridicule to achieve their success. If they could succeed, then why can't we?

Taking risks leads to trying again. As we try again, we do not attach our worth to our do-over. It is an unrealistic expectation to think we will always hit the nail on the head on the first try.

No doesn't mean *never* unless we allow it to. Every *no* can lead you down a different avenue that will likely turn out better than you originally thought.

Realistically we will need to make several do-over's and try different things before we settle on what works best to achieve the desired result, trying again means looking at failure with eyes of opportunity for success.

Failure has been given a bad rap. We view failure as a permanent state, as something inherently wrong with us. It is the very opposite. Failure brings the second, third, and fourth chances we need to accomplish a job well done. It is the opportunity to improve our ability and reasoning. Failure brings us that much closer to success. Without the failures that precede us trying again, we would not discover more efficient way of doing things. Successful techniques and advances in farming, canning, sewing, teaching, air travel, writing, technology, and so many other things would not be the benefit they are to our society today had failure not come first.

I have Nigerian Dwarf goats on my homestead. No matter how I fed my goats, there always seemed to be wasted hay. This was getting expensive. All I saw was money being thrown out and trampled on. Despite popular belief, goats don't eat anything and everything, and dirty hay is never a first choice. Plus, it is not healthy for them to eat hay that they may have soiled on.

It was frustrating for me, but I kept raking up all that hay and throwing it out onto the hillside. The next season, I noticed growth out on the hillside where I was throwing everything I was scooping out of their pens. It was turning into a beautiful hayfield! Everything I had considered to be a waste and an expensive failure was actually going to save me money.

This experience with the hay taught me firsthand about beginning to look differently at failure. Failure was the compost used to grow my hay field. When we look at failure differently, it will naturally breed a newer, healthier, and stronger life. Recovering self-worth means continuing to try.

Take Action

What are three things you gave up on?

1)_____

_____

_____

_____

_____

What can you do differently this time around?

_____

_____

_____

_____

_____

Set a start date to try again._____

2)_____

_____

_____

_____

_____

What can you do differently this time around?

_____

_____

_____

_____

_____

Set a start date to try again._____

3)_____

_____

_____

_____

_____

What can you do differently this time around?

_____

_____

_____

_____

_____

What is the start date to try again._____

Chapter 18

Self-Worth Is
Taking Risks Knowing You Can Handle the
Outcome

Taking healthy risks is important as you begin to trust the person you are. When we trust ourselves, we are not looking for the approval of others; rather we are embracing and utilizing our uniquely and strategically given talents. The Designer knew what we were to accomplish, so He intricately wove all that was necessary inside the tapestry of our hearts, drive, and creativity to complete the assignments (2 Pet. 1:3).

We've all heard that no two snowflakes are the same. If the Designer made snowflakes so very different from one another, each possessing its own beauty that would eventually melt away into nonexistence, how much more would He make His special creations, who will live for eternity, to be brilliantly different from one another? When celebrating uniqueness, I'm not talking about the pride of self or other man-made differences that stray from the Designer's intent for humanity. I'm speaking solely of the different dreams we have, the dream inside of each one of us that can only be accomplished by following our personal blueprints. And who would know this direction better than the One who created us for this current time? So, it is imperative to let your negative voice and the voice of the naysayer go unheeded as you take risks. We mustn't allow ourselves to embrace someone else's direction for us—we may begin to hold on to their direction so tightly that it starts to whisper, sowing seeds of self-doubt, and ultimately, we may allow it to change our course of action.

Not everyone is going to be for you during your endeavors, and nor should they be. The dream is yours, not theirs. The vision is there for you to make manifest, not for them.

There is nothing wrong with seeking counsel. In fact, the Bible says wisdom is found in a multitude of counselors (Prov. 11:14).

When we seek counsel, we do it while maintaining the right to receive it or dismiss it. It doesn't mean they are horrible people, or you just want what you want, or the counsel wasn't good. It simply means that after you have weighed the counsel before God, it wasn't the right path for your particular mission. Then give yourself permission to trust your instinct of what God is calling you to do. It's just like when you are eating chicken. You keep the meat and toss out the bones.

You can take the necessary risks because you are resourceful enough to use even unexpected outcomes as opportunities to learn, grow, and make allowances and changes until you meet success face to face.

Take Action

In the space below write down your dream—not how you are going to get there, just the big picture and what the end result would bring. How would you or others be affected? Use more paper if needed. Everyone has a dream.

_____

_____

_____

_____

_____

_____

_____

_____

_____

_____

_____

_____

_____

_____

_____

_____

_____

According as his divine power hath given unto us all things that pertain unto life and godliness, through the knowledge of him that hath called us to glory and virtue.
—2 Peter 1:3

Where no counsel is, the people fall: but in the multitude of counsellors there is safety.
—Proverbs 11:14

Chapter 19

Self-Worth Is Setting Goals

Not long after I started attending church, a new couple had come one Sunday to visit my church. All through the church service, I was trying to talk myself into asking them over for dinner. I was so preoccupied with asking them that the message not only was preached but had ended, and to this day I couldn't tell you what it was about. My thoughts were on how my house wasn't clean, my furniture wasn't very nice, my children and I didn't have very nice clothes, and food was extremely limited. What would they think of me?

I finally mustered up just enough courage after the service to ask. I went up to the woman and said, "So, you want to come to dinner?" I didn't even do it with a smile or make it welcoming. Right about that time her husband walked up, and she looked at him and said, "Hun, I think we just received a dinner invite." They came that night, and we all had the best time. My fears in that situation proved to be invalid.

Recovering self-worth and setting goals go hand in hand. When I speak of goals, I'm not necessarily referring to five- and ten-year career-goal plans, although they are important. The goals I'm talking about are the little things that are not so little when you're struggling with self-worth. They can be practicing interacting with others on a personal level or reaching out to others and letting them know how you really feel. These are a couple of those not-so-little goals you can make if you're struggling with self-worth. In order to reach out, we have to let go of those fears of not being heard and not being validated. As we have already had these experiences many times before, the thought of reaching out in this manner can be enough to send us running for cover. This is why we set little goals when learning to let others in on the real us.

Inviting someone to lunch or going for a walk with a neighbor are two great ways to create opportunities to practice allowing the real you to be present. Taking the risk of being known is scary. By focusing on the little goals, we will strengthen our core selves, and in time we will be able to accomplish the not-so-little goals.

Another one of those not-so-little goals could be to lend a helping hand. This will require laying aside your fear momentarily to be there for someone else. Easier said than done, yes, but it can be done. Thoughts of sugar plums are not dancing in our heads as we think of offering our help to someone and risking doing something wrong or being found out. Thoughts like these keep us from even trying. We try very hard to not allow anyone to see how useless we (falsely believe) we are. To put ourselves out there to help goes against everything we have worked so hard to hide. This fear leads us right back to attaching our worth to our mistakes.

We have to remind ourselves that our value is not determined by our mistakes, but rather has been determined by the Designer.

Other not-so-little goals are the day-to-day business we should practice attending to. Doing some things throughout the day makes for a more enjoyable and fulfilling life. These can include household chores, running errands, exercising, and so on.

I found it rewarding to write down three things that I would like to accomplish in the day, and then I did them. It is empowering to check off items on the to-do-list. It is a gentle reminder of what we are capable of.

As we continue to follow through with the commitments we made to ourselves (like our to-do list), it builds confidence. As we master some of our day-to-day tasks, we start to believe we can accomplish other goals. What is accomplishing goals but a way to increase self-worth? Self-worth increases because you believe in yourself. Self-worth evolves even more than achieving your goals; it knows the value you bring to others because of your creativity, your ideas, your ability, your kindness—it's the person you are. We all have different talents. Recovering self-worth means not comparing yourself to others (see chapter 10).

Your goals provide direction for you. We let go of being happenstance people. We live on purpose. Living on purpose involves reviewing our goals and tackling them one by one. Let's face it: some of the goals we have to set to get to our overall desire may not be fun, but they are necessary. This is when we force ourselves to honor the commitment we made to ourselves. Just because we have this wonderful plan or idea doesn't mean it is going to be a bed of roses all the time. We have to fight through self-doubt for what we want. We have to silence the negative voices that say that it's too hard, too scary, or that we are incapable.

We never listen to the voice that says just give up. No, we are more than conquerors in Christ Jesus (Rom. 8:37). This is the time to remember that you are not alone. Everyone who sets goals also has to fight through to attain them. This is life.

Setting goals reinforces purpose in our lives and serves as a reminder that other people don't determine our outcome, we do. To reach our full potential, we have to take responsibility for our choices and actions. I understand how life can throw us a curve ball, but the Designer has already determined that we can even knock the curve ball out of the park. We were created for good things. But it's up to us to seek it out and write it out (Prov. 29:18; Hab. 2:2).

Take time to write out your goals for recovering your self-worth. A helpful acronym for setting goals is the SMART tool.

Specific: What do you want? Don't be broad or leave room for interpretation: for example, "I want more self-esteem" (this one is too vague). What would having more self-esteem be like? "I share my opinions; I go for my goals; I don't allow others to treat me poorly" (this one is more specific).

Measurable: How long will it take to achieve your goal of gaining self-esteem? Give yourself a realistic time frame.

Attainable: We know other people who have a healthy self-image. Therefore, we know it is something that can be accomplished.

Realistic: What are you willing to do to achieve your goals? For example, take a class; hire a life coach, read a book on the subject, and so on.

Time bound: Set a deadline for when you want to complete a specific goal. What self-esteem goals are you working on that you want to have accomplished by the set time?

Every step reached within your goals builds confidence. Every time you make a mistake and get back up, this too builds confidence.

Take Action

On a separate piece of paper write out your goals using the SMART goal outline. Take your time. Remember, this is not written in stone. Goals do change as accomplishments happen. This doesn't have to be perfect. Try to put down a couple of sentences in each category.

Nay, in all these things we are more than conquerors through him that loved us.
—Romans 8:37

Where there is no vision, the people perish: but he that keepeth the law, happy is he.
—Proverbs 29:18

And the LORD answered me and said, Write the vision, and make it plain upon tablets, that he may run that readeth it.
—Habakkuk 2:2

Chapter 20

Self-Worth Is
Good Hygiene and Personal Appearance

I can still hear my mother telling us to make sure we had on clean underwear in case we got into an accident. "Stay prepared" was her motto. When we leave the house, we never know what the day may bring. This could be the day we meet Mr. or Mrs. Right. It could be the day that we are chosen for something. Whatever the day may bring, taking thirty minutes at the beginning of your day to love on yourself makes a difference in how you carry yourself and how others perceive you. Sometimes we need to go back to the basic learning tools, the infamous checklist. A checklist is great in helping us remain accountable to ourselves. It serves as a reminder of what we have decided to do. Every time you check an item off the list, it gives you a feeling of accomplishment. No matter how big or small, you accomplished something that you had committed to do. Personal hygiene can be placed on that list. Here's an example list:

√ Showered
√ Combed hair
√ Brushed teeth
√ Put on clean clothes

Taking care of our bodies is another action we practice as we recover self-worth. Personal hygiene says, "I care about myself." Not many people want to be around someone who has an odor that can be helped, whether it is body or breath. Poor hygiene can be used as a self-protection device. We know that if we carry ourselves a certain way, we can keep people at a distance. We do not want to risk being hurt. We tell ourselves that it is our very self that people do not want to be around, when it really is our defense mechanism that they don't want to be around. Recovering self-worth requires dropping the once-needed artillery and taking the time to put our best foot forward by practicing good hygiene.

Take Action

Let's hit that checklist again. For the first week, make a commitment to practice good hygiene two days out of the week. For the second week, practice three times. The third week practice three times again. For the fourth week, practice four times that week. For the fifth week, practice five times, and the sixth week, seven times. Be sure to check it off every time you honor your commitment to yourself. This is used for accountability, not condemnation.

Mon	Tues	Wed	Thurs	Fri	Sat	Sun

Chapter 21

Self-Worth Is
Looking in the Mirror and Smiling

Standing there as I stared in the mirror, I had to smile. For the first time I saw art, a masterpiece. I didn't always feel this way. Thinking back, I remember the day a friend grabbed me by the hand and took me to the bathroom mirror. She told me very firmly to look at myself and say "I love you." I couldn't do it. I just cried. There wasn't anything about me I found worth loving, not my looks or what was on the inside. But on this particular day I had a pleasant reaction toward my reflection. At that moment I knew I could no longer blame society for how it portrayed beauty. It carries a very limited view of beauty. How can you look at the sunset and say, "That is true beauty," and fail to see the beauty in the ocean or the mountainside? I'm sure you can't. Every creation carries its own natural beauty. No one stroke of the brush makes the art a masterpiece.

All too often, we size up people by their outside. I know there is physical attraction and that there is outer beauty, but the true beauty of a person takes time to see. I could also no longer blame others for the perception I had toward myself. Through becoming a willing participant in recovering my self-worth by taking action, I found that the negative talk toward myself naturally began to fade. The authentic words began to peek through the darkness and overshadow the negative with the light of self-love. As I stood there studying myself, I began to see compassion, intelligence, creativity, kindness, peace, strength, honesty, trustworthiness, and a spirit of encouragement. I noticed my physical appearance as well, but when it came down to beauty, it wasn't the things that could be immediately seen by the human eye that caused me to smile. It was my growing character that I found beauty in. It was my attributes, what I contributed to my sphere of influence. It was my ability to love all of me that made me smile.

Take Action

It's time to return to the mirror. Every day for seven days, repeat these affirmations. After you have completed the seven days, do seven more. Continue with these or others like them until you see the incredible masterpiece you are.

I am dearly loved by the Designer.
I am fearfully and wonderfully made.
I have a purpose and destiny to fulfill.
I do not strive for perfection. I strive to do my best.
Fear no longer holds me back.
I am more than capable to do this thing called life.
Yesterday is gone. Today I will live.
I give myself permission to enjoy life.
I am gifted and talented.
I matter. I have value. I am lovable.
I am not alone. Everyone makes mistakes.
I will continue to grow and learn.
The Designer Himself looked at me and called me good.

The LORD your God is in your midst, a mighty one who will save; he will rejoice over you with gladness; he will quiet you by his love; he will exult over you with loud singing.
—Zephaniah 3:17 ESV

For I know the thoughts that I think toward you, saith the LORD, thoughts of peace, and not of evil, to give you an expected end.
—Jeremiah 29:11

For God hath not given us the spirit of fear; but of power, and of love, and of a sound mind.
—2 Timothy 1:7

And God saw everything that he had made, and behold, it was very good. And the evening and the morning were the sixth day.
—Genesis 1:31

This is an amazing time as you continue on your journey to recovering self-worth. It is my sincere hope that you, dear reader, will also look in the mirror and smile.

Enjoy the journey!
—Jeannie

www.ingramcontent.com/pod-product-compliance
Lightning Source LLC
Chambersburg PA
CBHW031522040426
42445CB00009B/356